YAHOOZE! Scamming the Scammer

John Robert Chaney III

READ THIS FIRST, PLEASE:

DISCLAIMER: <u>I do not recommend this activity for the general public</u>. Social media scammers are criminals and are ruthless, desperate people who do not respect laws. The games that I play with them are not suggested for other people. This is because they could endanger someone's life if things do not go as planned.

If you ever are contacted by someone on social media you do not know, I recommend closing the message, and blocking them. Don't communicate with people that you do not know on any social media platform, through email, or any other method. Just DON'T DO IT.

The main takeway here is that 100% of the time, if a stranger contacts me, the reason is that they want to scam money from me. That is the only reason they would do that. The best thing to do, in my opinion, is if a message pops up of someone you do not know in real life, **close it, and block that person**. That way, they cannot track you down, they cannot get your money, and there is almost no chance that something bad can happen.

I do not want that for anyone, and <u>I do not recommend giving any information or money to ANYONE on the internet</u>. **That is not safe**. Don't do that. And if you do get scammed, remember: it is not the fault of the author of this book. The author of this book clearly recommends staying clear of people on the internet that you do not know in real life to be trustworthy people.

READ THIS PART NEXT:

This book contains some profanity and sexual dialogue. It is not for anyone considered a "minor" or "underage" by whatever method their locality defines it. I set the age range up to the maximum to keep minors out, but unfortunately, minors always find a way… (at least I did…)

First Edition

Key to Abbreviations:

F = Facebook

FF = Facebook Friend (people who are only friends through F, and have not corresponded outside in the real world)

M = Facebook Messenger (the F system that allows FF to communicate by text through the F system), or it refers to a text sent through the F message system

R = Request to be friends on F

Message status codes on page 2: c, Cl, s

FS = Facebook scammers (also includes Facebook prostitutes, and other criminals)

S = general term for a Facebook scam or internet scam

M = mark, a term for someone who is the intended target of a FS

Who is the Modern Facebook Scammer (FS)? The answer is: anyone. They exist in every country in the world, and are impossible to find or imprison. If the police or authorities do catch a FS it is usually not because of S. They are usually arrested for dealing drugs, stealing, prostitution, murder, violence, or another crime. The crimes they commit occur in conditions of secrecy.

2

The secrecy may be the main reason this continues. The ancient promise of technology turned out to be a complete lie. Technology does not enhance the world in any possible way. Computers only create more paperwork for businesses and institutions. With more files on computer systems, the legal system has come to realize that with the stroke of a key, information can be changed and falsified. Since misinformation has the potential to be in a volume that exceeds numerical count, the human race has realized that the information that exists on hard drives is not worth sorting out. In the end, people can only rely on what they can track on paper because other sources of information are subject to hacking, malicious manipulation or were inaccurate in the first place. What is left appears to be of no value, which is a dung pile of bytes.

It is from this kind of murky and vile sewage where FS emerge. They gather together in small gangs, and usually have weapons nearby. There was once a time where batches of them seemed to have been discovered in impoverished places such as African countries, or marginally stable places such as former Soviet countries. Eventually the slimy ways of greedy people unable to compose coherent sentences moved across borders. It was an inevitable change that was likely brought on by the very people who were victimized by it.

That's right. There is no such thing as theft by a willing victim. A consensual crime is an oxymoron. Americans especially do not want anyone to know what has happened when they have donated their money to a stranger, and received nothing in return. The American culture works in such a way as to prevent most people from admitting that they have been Yahoozed. Yahoozed is a term for someone getting scammed by another person on the internet. The main breeding territory for scams at this point in time is F. The number of profiles far exceeds the number of people that any population census has counted.

The reason for this is because usually FS operate multiple screen computer systems with multiple users on the other end at the same time. FS know that many times a person will not have money or will not be motivated to send them money, so they try to diversify their efforts. This is where I come in.

My objective is to cut out a slice of their time, whenever possible. As much as I can get, I will take. My methods are as diverse as the mood grabs me at that time. I have taken many a FS down the aisle for very long periods of time, and just after the priest is finished reading the portion of vows I am to affirmate, I decide instead to depart. The next day, I find the same FS and restart the whole thing.

The way I figure it, every moment that I can attract a FS and keep them busy, then I have the potential of making the world a better place. If I can slow a FS down by distracting them, that means that they are not getting money from an M. If they are unsuccessful with an M, they have less money to buy heroin, guns or some other type of criminal scheme designed to enrich the scum of the earth on the backs of honest, hardworking people. It appears that I finally have a victorious book to write, and I don't have to apologize for it. Thank you FS for making me rich. Your stupidity is humorous, tragic and I have no sympathy for you. The reader can only benefit from this book.

The only sad thing about this book is that the information will only protect people for so long. FS will eventually read my book, get better at the depraved craft, or find other ways to get money without earning it. There is only one way that has ever existed where people get money without earning it, which is through crime. There is no upside for anyone who is engaged in crime, and fortunately, we have a God of Heaven who will not change that. I like the way He thinks!

Other reasons why this book will become obsolete is that as I mentioned, the victims most of the time do not talk about their own victimhood. Once in a while a story comes across on the news, but a sound byte or even a full story rarely lacks any meaningful details that could help the public. The last reason is that these people are experts and it is all they do, or can do, in between jail sentences. It is hard to beat Mike Tyson in the ring. I'm a tough guy, athletic and energetic, but beating Mike Tyson challenges even the best fighters in the world. That is the problem with criminals. If they spend all their time to improve their craft, even authorities who are actively pursuing them are playing a game of catch-up. What is worse is the enormous sums of money that is spent trying to capture, and put on trial, people who did not make it past the 6th grade or less. FS are not intelligent people most of the time, but the advantage they have over the M is a desperate dedication to activities that will condemn them on earth and in the afterlife. But God's decision in those matters is always correct. His justice, as He pulls back on the lever that opens the trap door underneath them and sends them into eternal torment, puts a smile on my face. Because sooner or later, if you ask any criminal, God WILL PULL BACK ON THAT LEVER!

My job is to show what is going on right now, and how a person can avoid trouble and how, if they are so inclined to end the problem. The first thing to do is never to send money across the internet to a person. Just don't. If a family member needs money, mail them a check. But sending money to people is a bad idea anyway.

If a person is in a bad spot in life, the reason that nobody wants to accept is the fact that God sometimes puts them there. The reason He does that is because they might need to learn a lesson or make some kind of change. That's what prison is for: rehabilitation. A person who returns to prison has not learned their lesson, so it's back to 2nd grade again. If the old saying is "crime doesn't pay", they are half-right. Criminals eventually receive free money from the M. And fighting crime is a good source of legal income for people to develop a rewarding career from. They have my respect, the police, first responders, doctors, nurses, and the military. They are worth much more than their salaries, in my humble opine.

Sometimes when a person arrives at the bad spot in life, God's main goal is for them to turn to Him when the situation is dire. If they do, He solves their problem and they see a miracle, which they cannot understand or explain, and their Godless friends will never believe the event. God's mission in that situation was not to save the Godless at that time usually. He could care less what they think. Me too. But the person who repents, changes their ways and looks to the Father for forgiveness, becomes a person who can be saved, and can even prosper through legal means while on earth. Unfortunately, the group of people that make said change is not big enough. Sometimes, skepticism screams that such a population of the reformed is nearly zero, globally. That's a bad day.

FS are so bad at what they do in recent days, I have a tremendous pity for them. But I have much more interest in the overall benefit to society that I donate by putting them in painful headlocks. Sometimes I wish I could find a FS and spy on them, at a distance. Where do they operate? What car do they drive? What can I find out about who they live and what kinds of other ancillary crimes are they actively pursuing? I've always wondered if I could catch them in a drug or weapon deal, and report it or somehow make it go wrong. Of course, physical investigations are not possible. But the superficial investigations of a profile are enough to know who are the bad people.

All a Facebook user needs to identify is a small amount of common sense, and I wish more people had it. I can be optimistic on the other hand: you are reading this book. This book will contain much information about the subject in order to help the public avoid scams. My prerogative is to starve them of money, the FS. I won't be able to do it without your help. Anyone who does this must do it in exactly the way I depict. For the moment, let's investigate the basics.

1. There may have been a society when attractive women found strange men to fall in love with, but

that mythological place and time has not existed in my life and in this world, and is certainly not happening right now. Women, unfortunately do not do that. Maybe Sting or Charlie Sheen effortlessly had women fling themselves at them, I don't know. But I am not those guys, I do not know anything that has not been printed about them, and of that information, have not read much of it. All that's necessary to know is that when I get an instant message on messenger, if I do not recognize the name, it's a red flag already.

2. Keep this rule in mind: if you detect one red flag, it has been my experience that there are more mines in that minefield. Rarely if ever, do I even need to open a profile page on F to make a determination if someone is a scammer. A stranger who contacts me out of nowhere has only found me because they were searching. Usually it is the photograph of a model or porn star taken from the internet. Once in a blue moon, I can recognize the picture of certain models. That's how lazy FS are.

3. All of those first two items are enough to detect a scammer, but a stranger who says "hi" to me and is the picture of a model or porn actress, whether I've seen the picture before or not, makes a total of two red flags. Now the odds of this person being a scammer have doubled in less than a second. I usually do not need to know any more, before I start working an angle to waste their time, which benefits the world and slows their inevitable scam.

4. The profile is always a dead giveaway. If the name is in a Cyrillic alphabet, such as Russian, now there is nearly a 100% chance this person is a scammer. A model with a Russian name is always a scammer, especially if she contacts me first.

5. Since I am a guy, I have no interest in making friends with strange dudes in distant places, so for me, if a guy contacts me, it's a no go. But I will let them contact me and become friends so I can waste their time. Especially if they send me a message first.

6. If I dig deeper into the profile for more information, the absence of information is a major red flag. FS assume that a guy will only be concerned about the M that is going on right at that moment with the FS. They might be right, except when it comes to someone out to eat the time of the rabble. Most FS don't fill out very much information on their profiles. Why bother?

7. An FS is looking to get a chunk of money out of an M and disappear. They want the money yesterday, and most of them have a heroin habit that requires it so they don't get dope sick. They work hard to develop strategies to manipulate money out of people.

8. Their main angle is to make a single guy think that a woman is in love with him. Let's take a deeper look at a recent conversation I had:

A hot chick approached me, claiming to be from Texas. I had never actually been on Texas soil very much. Once time I passed through in a van before and also I did see the inside of DFW en route to Seattle in 2005. That cheerful crowd of friends somehow did not likely produce the woman of whom I was easily an object of affection.

As we spoke, after a few M, I told her how frustrated I was that I couldn't get a date, and that every time I talked to a woman, she disappeared. This FS said, I will stay with you. So we continued to talk, and that FS made me realize the whole plot. She said she would love to see me for a date this weekend. I told her to come on down. Then she laid it out in simple terms: I need 40% of the cost of the airline ticket.

That was interesting. Was I worth 40% of $500 = $200? Immediately I let her know that her love must not be real if she needed a deposit for the beginning of our long lasting courtship. Then she asked for $25. I could not make this up, it defies logic. My original intention was to copy the entire dialogue, but among the multitude of scammers, I couldn't find it.

I decided to offer her a smaller amount. I made her wait a very long time as I pretended to count the cash in my wallet. I counted $7. I didn't actually count the money, I just sat there for a while, and repeatedly sent her useless messages to distract her, such has:

> hang on
> wait a sec
> seems like I had more…
> is this bill counterfeit
> somebody's at the door
> do you like cheetos

So I gave her the bad news which was that our marriage had to be temporarily put on hold, since I couldn't send her the $7. She became upset, and asked "why not?" My reason was that I didn't know how to do it. She started to explain it to me, and midway through, stopped. I shut down F at that point, knowing she was on to me, and now on to the next dude. It hurt, the fact that I couldn't distract her from a victim for longer, but on the bright side, I thought it was a good attempt for the first time out.

Then I had a bad day, and it dawned on me that I could take all my aggression out on the FS. So that happened more than once. I usually do not curse, but I realized that my anger didn't seem to have an upper limit, at least not that day. Here are some of the choice things I said to some FS:

> you are scum
> die

piece of garbage is what you are
if I see you on the street my fist will go
through your head like a stone, and you won't see
me coming
etc.

There was a lot more cruelty and brutality, but then I realized that if they became afraid, which they were not usually, then they'd just switch ids, or close out my M. I figured that I'd make better traction by being nice and taking them down the altar. Before I became convinced that way would work better, I decided to do other weird strategies.

One conversation proved to me that I had deadly accuracy at spotting a FS without looking at a profile. A hot model, claiming to be from Los Angeles sent me an M one day. I knew it was going to be a romance angle she was going to work. I keep saying "she" but unfortunately, as Toto pulled back the curtain revealing the diminutive wizard in similar fashion, most FS are not always women. But these dudes in back alley boiler room operations can find obscure pictures of models and post them on profiles. Profiles which usually do not contain any other information.
Think about that. A hot chick from Los Angeles does not want her contact information on F. What are the odds of that? The answer is zero. That's because hot chicks out there are usually actresses or models, and they depend on PUBLICITY. That how hot women, the lion's share of them, make money in southern California. They want to be famous and they know that the more people that know about them, the more they have the chance to meet someone who can give them a breakthrough role in a film, find a better agent, and move up beyond the working poor who slum around studios in the area in a futile attempt to be the next star. Fame and publicity are the stock and trade of celebrities. When studios, writers, directors, producers, and casting agents start to forget about them, they lose their star power, and they jeopardize their career, or never get it off the ground.

A hot chick is not going to contact someone who lives a vast distance away, under nearly any circumstance, except in the case where she already knew that person, for instance if it was her hometown, like Iowa Falls or Buffalo. If she wanted to get a date, she would hang out in L.A. and it would not take long for a man to make a pass at her, even if she was only marginally attractive. And many times I would argue that maybe there is not a woman under the age of 50 or so who can't at least get sex from some guy somewhere. If she gets a guy to have sex with her once, which doesn't require much effort on her part beyond just waiting, I feel certain he'd at least come back a second time if she was a reasonable person. I would!

But many men cannot deal with their loneliness, and when a hot chick suddenly messages them out of the blue, they lose perspective. Unfortunately, far too often she has a way with her words that get the man to send her money. Then most of the time, I suspect, she vanishes into the haze. He goes back to look at her profile after sending her 40% of a plane ticket, and the profile has been removed. This cycle happens one the minute around the world. It's nauseating.

What words did she say to him that made him send the money? I don't know. When FS approach me to start their angle of attack, I have always been keen to see how they do it, but apparently, have not found a way to motivate me to send money yet. I never have sent money across F. One time I had the app open and I hit the button accidentally, but there was another screen after it that I did not recognize, and so I just closed it. I had never had it connected to my account, so it couldn't have sent money anyway, which is intentional on my part.

I don't know if there is a certain phrase that they have discovered that is a silver bullet. Every time I have encountered FS, it seems like I try to be friendly for a while, and if I continue, they usually ask me to "send a card". The first time this happened, I assumed that they meant some kind of prepaid credit card that gas stations and stores sell. Knowing that already, that scammer, (which was not the one from L.A.) started to demand it repeatedly, with anger. Then she disappeared.

The L.A. hot girl was ok except that she had bad grammar. Bad grammar is sometimes ok on texts and M, but since the odds were good that I was dealing with a starlet or media personality, those people make their money by reading. People who read a lot, usually value certain grammatical rules, and having learned them over decades, often do not want to throw them away by developing bad habits on texts. That would risk their plans to be famous, if they lost the ability to read scripts in order to text the guy in Columbus, Georgia who drives a farm truck she has never met before.

Then as the convo continued with the hot L.A. girl continued, she made a slight miscalculation. I asked her, "How is the weather in LA right now?" Her answer, "What is this LA you speak of"? I wondered if she was one of the worst scammers I'd ever dealt with. But that was good to start with the idiots and work my way up, in order to later nail the marlins or whales even.

Unfortunately, when I discovered that all her efforts were focused on committing an illegal activity that she was not yet proficient with, I felt an immense sadness for her soul. I just decided that time to let her off the hook. I might have continued with her a little bit, but my heart wasn't in it. This worm I decided not to smash because the bulk of her pain and misery was nearly inevitable and soon forthcoming.

If that was an isolated event of incompetence from a FS, then I would have doubled down to fight them with more fury later on. I did not usually get angry because sometimes I discovered that I could come up with some wacky conversations. This one is copied exactly:

FS: Hello Handsome how are you doing, Thanks for accepting my friend questing ??

John ::: i love accepting your friend questing

FS:
Okay
I'm doing great as well, It nice hearing from you John
Where do you come from??

John ::
I emerged from Antarctica, breaking through the ice (I made a
typo it was supposed to be "breaking")

FS:
Oh okay that's nice of you
Well I'm Joyce from Texas Dallas but lost my parent so i
earlier went to live with my gran mom in Ghana and i really
love my gran mom much because she was the one that has
taking care of me,

John ::
oh that was so nice of you to travel to ghana to your gran mom

FS:
Yes as well,and are you married with kids??

John ::
yes I have 34 wives, and 118 children and 334 grandchildren
i'm looking for a few more wives today

FS:
Okay
I have never been married with no kids, And I'm here looking
for my soulmate someone i can trust him with all my heart,
someone that can care for us and make our dream true

John ::
when will i be able to get you pregnant?

FS:
Okay
So are you also ready to be in a long term relationship?

John ::
nah i just like populating the world, honestly. i like moving my
sperm into an egg

FS:
Oh okay
How old are you??

John ::
I'm 138
        I realize the conversation went sideways, but I think the
reader can benefit from the conversation. First of all, she was
the one, this hot model, who initiated the M. Red flag number
one. Next, her opener was so bad: Thanks for accepting my
friend questing ?? What kind of native English speaker would
type that? The answer is none. It's just not how English
speakers think or talk. Red flag number two.
        If someone from the UK or Australia, or any distant
place that speaks English contacted me, it would not read like
that at all. I don't want to say a lot about English grammar
right now because that would have the potential to make it
easy on a scammer who lucked into my book. But it is my
opinion that most scammers do not read too often. Unless it
results in obtaining heroin. The last time I read Bukowski's
"Factotum", I did not end up getting heroin. Of course, I could
be an anomaly.
        Scammers do not speak English very well because
they usually do not complete enough school. Their life
situations are too harsh for that. They are impoverished,
hungry, scared, and often transient. They usually grew up in
tough conditions that are much worse than it is in America,
and for that, I feel sad. However, I learned one interesting
thing the last time I watched the softcore porn classic
"Emmanuelle Around the World", which was the line, "Justice
is no friend to compassion." Of course if they had said that
the sky is green instead during that scene, I'd have
remembered it just as well. And believed it too!

14

Justice cannot exist in places where there is too much subjectivity, pity or relative ethics. Relative ethics is a concept that people who do not know God invented in order to create flexible rules in order to achieve some kind of evil goal. A discussion of relative ethics is not relevant for this book, as it deserves its own book. Hmmmm, I'm getting an idea. I digress again.

Justice is what separates order from anarchy, hard work from scams and good from evil. Although many legislative portions of governments around the world cannot get it right in every case that enters the courtroom nor in every law that a well-intentioned representative hatched in order to solve a problem, I do believe that there is a foundation of moral justice in the world. It works most of the time because the people who run it usually want it to work the right way, which is for the guilty to be behind bars and for the innocent to be compensated for the trouble they often did not deserve. I think God places solid people to run things and the Bible reflects that in the words of the Apostle Paul, the genius. Thousands of years on, the cat and mouse game usually results in the cat eating his dinner.

Other problems also existed in the M I was just talking about. Notice how eager she is in the second time I've ever communicated with this stranger in my life. Does that match up with the way most people react in a modern day society plunging into ignorance and irrelevance? No. Usually when I speak to a stranger, which I don't usually do because the results are so unpredictable, they seem to want to escape. So I let them. There is an atmosphere here in America of fear, that seems to underlie every interaction, familiar or otherwise. I've rarely ever met a stranger in America, which is where I've lived all my life, who wants to talk to me. Most people are too busy, buried into their cell phones, or can't take their mind off of the latest John Robert Chaney III book. Who could blame them for the latter? I like their taste.

Self-referencing jokes aside, society has lost the picture on normal relationships because too many people are focused on handheld smart phones. What is happening there for them that is more important than their environment? The answer is, everything. If they can get a "like", a "FF" or some other form of false validation, it almost seems as if these kinds of things are as important as mitochondrial energy in the cardiac muscle. But they are not.

I wish I could write a book on the pitfalls of the internet or social media. Wait, I'm deep on the inside of one now. For some reason, the human race has placed a value on things that have an amount of value that in my opinion costs more than it is worth, by parsecs. A parsec is a distance used in astronomy that cannot be traversed by humans. A good example of that distance is from our solar system to the nearest star that IS NOT our sun, Proxima Centauri. It's, of course, NOT an exact parsec by any stretch, but it's so far away, that it will NEVER BE REACHED BY HUMANS. ("Avatar" fans, reread that last sentence until it's understood.)

There is more than one pitfall. The human body is not responding well to smart phones in my opinion. The head and neck do not usually stay pain free in the forward-bent position which reading apps requires. This will lead, in the long run, to a situation where nerve impulses originating from the brain to the body, possibly as close as the eyes, will start to slow down, being choked. I'm not trying to say that over time people will completely lose the ability to think, but I am not sure sometimes. If the nerve impulses from the brain to the body are unaffected, humans might survive longer, but still there is a vast amount of peril that this addiction is putting before us in unprecedented directions. The worst one is that nobody cares.

Some of this peril is the fact that in our quest for validations that have ZERO potential for profit or value. Of the miniscule financial resources that are available to most of the hoi polloi, sometimes the seasoned scammer has the wind at his back as he seeks a man to put on him a wedding veil. And upon receiving it, the M discovers a knife into his back as he turns to pick up the ring on the pillow from the child beside the altar. She laughs as she twists and rotates the knife with the finesse of a Los Angeles actress who can't find California.

Her face looks more like the Joker than Angelina Jolie in that moment. Where was the love, the hope, the future? It didn't change: it's right there, in your back!

Another pitfall is complete speculation on my part, if there are not any studies out to confirm my fear. Humans, because of their constant focus in a downward position on a small area are losing their peripheral vision. It happens constantly; people cross the street while texting during rush hour, people drive while texting on the freeway, and if they are not texting, they are using some kind of app that otherwise is ruining their field of vision. Is this a problem? My answer is yes. It is that very peripheral vision that gives them the illusion of safety as they take their eyes away from environmental hazards. Like all muscles in humans and animals (Humans ARE NOT animals!), peripheral vision will atrophy over time as the range of sight decreases for smart phone users.

Also I am expecting a large decline in the birth rate because of social media. This is happening because men and women no longer flirt with each other in public spaces anymore. Instead, they are searching out across the internet to connect with Nigerians across the Atlantic posing as actresses who cannot find the entertainment capital of the world. In the old days, every so often a man and a woman who had never met before could hook up in a bar, and sometimes a birth was the result. Now that no longer happens, but it is much worse, which is that people are isolating themselves into small social groups filled with people who are not compatible for more than friendship. This trend of women "friend zoning" available men inside of their physical environment in favor of old friends they <u>do not</u> intend to mate with, seems like a collision course where everything goes wrong except the one collision that **needs** to happen: between a sperm and an egg.

Other times with scammers I really went for all kinds of insane narratives about whatever flash of inspiration I had at the moment. I got that idea from a movie called "Fletch" with Chevy Chase (1985). The movie is one of my all-time favorites, but what is really incredible is this scene where the police chief confronts Fletch (Chase) in the chief's office. He says to Fletch, "What do you do for a living?" Fletch at that moment knows he is in hot water, and no matter what he says, can't get out of trouble. So what does Fletch do in a no-win situation like that? He says something in an off-the-cuff manner that is not true, but seemed to be what popped in his brain in the moment. Fletch, a newspaper reporter responds with, "I'm a shepherd."

This is my approach to scammers. I just make up wild stories or anecdotes, and try to make them elaborate and ridiculous. Since the scammer operates in a high pressure environment that requires quotas most of the time, the boss of the illegal operation does not want to have to come over to the low-level scammer's computer to translate the English. Especially when the Nigerian scammer and his boss have an agreement, and the scammer's part of the deal was an understanding that the scammer was, in fact fluent in English. But rarely ever is this the case.

This is good for society. Since a scammer has spent their life surviving through all kinds of illegal means, studying English takes a back seat to making money by selling unmarked Uzis. That makes them much more readily identifiable. But they have another problem too, which is their utter laziness to do any kind of front work to seem credible! They won't do it! The first question they ask me is my name. The reason they do that is so they can copy and paste it once and a while. Are they slugs?

Criminals are not known for their persistence towards successful strategies in life. Since they find English too difficult to study on their own and don't look up profile information, why in the world do they think I'm going to send them money? This is the question that I cannot yet answer. I couldn't even be motivated by the Ukrainian man with the face of a female to send seven lousy dollars. And when I seemed resistant to the seven dollars, he gave up. Why not ask for six? He had already put in some time on this mark, which was me. Why didn't he offer oral sex which I would never receive anyway, for three dollars? I mean come on. Can this person generate enough willpower to force a fork towards their mouth with food on it, or not?

Using Fletch's method of "winging it", here's the dialogue:

FS::
Hello

John:
hi

FS::
How are you doing

John
good you?

FS::
Am fine
Where are you from

John:
where do you live?

FS::
Michigan in USA

John
ive never met a woman named (male name) before

FS::
It normal
Where are you from

John
yes how can i help?

FS::
How did you which to help me

FS::
Hello

John
a woman named "(man's name)" are you?

(at that moment the FS and his buddies had a good laugh, thinking their mark was stupid. Keep reading to see who gets the advantage.)

FS::
Yes dear
Did you like that

John
are you a tranny?

FS::
No
Why asking that

John
just a random question, no reason

FS::
Okay
What did you do for living

John
What did I do? Well, at my first job I riveted steel for Bushmills. (something I just made up.)

FS::
Okay

John
what is the problem?

FS::
Am still single
And you

John
I thought you wanted my resume? (the scammer didn't
know the word "resume", a common term in American
business, and he definitely did not want to look it up.)

FS::
I don't understand that

John
which part?
FS::
I want your resume as how

John
well, i was going to tell you about the job requirements
of Bushmills, but if you don't care, i can't force you.

FS::
Okay you can go ahead my dear

John
i mean, if you don't want it, then you don't have to have
it

FS::
I want it

John
ok so one day i was entering through the western
entrance, and Bob was there

(at this point, I had no idea what I'm going to say next, and I loved it!)
FS::
Okay

John
So I was asking him about the   10 unit production requirement, because the last hour of the day before, which was a Tuesday...

FS::
Okay

John
this is the cool part

FS::
Okay
That
Nice

John
so we got interrupted
and the arc welder was running low on amperage.
(the FS has no idea what I'm saying, other than just sitting there, wondering if

FS::
Okay

John
anyway, sorry. i'm working on a review for Life magazine

we tested it, and we could not get the power right. so they were trying to say production was low for a different reason
you know what i mean of course
right?
(this was a mistake I made. Never ask a "yes or no" question to these idiots. They will say yes, and wait until you're done, working other marks while this happens. Keep the volume of information lower than I did.)

FS::
Yes

John
so you know about amps?
hello?
(the FS gives up as usual, to the next mark. I hope his boss punished him for his incompetence. Otherwise, God will. I'll take the boss over God, any time.)

Here is the dialogue from another incompetent FS.

FS:
Hi

Me:
sup

FS:
Am fine and you

Me:
good

FS:
Nice to hear that

Me:

you heard it? (an FS will usually ignore dialogue they don't understand.)

FS:
Yea

Me:
and you live, where?

FS:
Malaysia, And you?

Me:
oh yes, I've been there many times! which part? (I was bluffing, and it worked!)
(very long pause)
(FS gives up in failure already.)

Me:
you can look on a map if you need help?
(he is now nordo)

Me:
it's a hard way to make an easy living, aint it?

FS:
Kuala Lumpur (obviously this one never took geography)

John:
try again
you take three hours to give me the wrong answer?
(then I started getting mad at the FS)
you are lazy and incompetant.
I don't think scamming people for money is going to be profitable for you.

FS
If you said so

John:
no i **wrote** it moron

The last line was something Doyle Brunson said, the poker player on a poker show one time. What it means is that poker players expect to make easy money sitting in an air-conditioned casino all day. Instead they get brutalized in the psychological tactics of newcomers that leaves them felted again. That turned out to be a phase in my development as a scam breaker: to pummel them into submission, into suicide or death if necessary. Since I would never be responsible for an actual killing of someone across a body of water, I wondered how bad I could make them feel about themselves. How far could it go? How ever far it could go, was where I wanted to take it. Maybe I could just work on their self-esteem for a while.

And then I realized that was an interesting strategy. If two guys are in a street fight, and I am fighting a battle against the FS, if my opponent is wearing a bandage, that is an area I will attempt to target with maximum force. It will cause more damage and pain, since the work is already started for me. Why be fair in this fight? If a scammer knew the perfect method that would hasten me to unload my wallet for them, they would take the shortest route to that point. So if they are actively trying to separate me from something that is legally and rightfully mine, then I should separate them from something even more crucial to their survival.

The thing that is mine is my money. The thing they need and do not have is confidence or self-esteem. They do not have that because they never earned it. It is a strange phenomena I have discovered about my spirituality, which is that God is not going to dole out confidence to people at a soup kitchen for free. It can only be earned. A criminal is a person who may have had some ideas of confidence when they were young, but by the time they are around high school age, have lost it. This is because they cycle through institutions, addictions, cruel people, and cannot make legal money. All the while, they have to live life in an environment that is dangerous and unpredictable. Once in a while a scammer is a rich boy who is bored, and has an evil streak that he uses to take on the challenge of a dialogue maze. This kind of person ultimately has an incredible fall from a stupendous height into the crags. He goes from the mansion into a near-concentration camp captivity, and is permanently marked. The hunter is now the hunted. The run of the mill criminal, or FS (who are one in the same), sees prison as a setback, a drug as an instant party and curses the God who created him as he recites a punchline to his joke.

Other dead giveaways are easily spotted, usually without much research. A female without a picture is normally a FS. That's because even if a female is not attractive for any reason, or lacks self-esteem, still she usually has enough courage to put a picture of herself on her profile. Without exception, every female that I have ever known in person, be it a family member or friend, has a selfie of their face on their profile. The reason they do this is because the people that I have known in my life are not criminals, and have nothing to hide. So what if they are not attractive? That does not detract from their value from my perspective. If they are family, their looks are not relevant to me. If they are old friends, I might entertain the idea of dating if the situation is good, but if my old friend from the old days does not have a picture on her profile, it probably means she has a severe drought of self-esteem or is not attractive. In either case, for me, it is a no go.
If her self-esteem is weak (an old female friend, I am speaking of), but she has a picture and isn't too hot, actually she'd have a better chance with me because looks are not the whole of a relationship. Some FS don't bother with posting pictures on their profiles either because it slows down their game or they had too many profiles with the same pictures out there! They try to spread out the pictures but once in a while they make a mistake, and that's why sometimes I can

recognize the pictures they put on the profiles. I may not know the name of the real life model who was photographed in the early 2000s or 1990s, but I know the picture.

What really makes the S bad for me is when an FS tries to pose as a military person. It makes me sick to reject the conversation of a hero, trying to fight for a country and sometimes merely wants some well-deserved validation from someone back home. I'm always happy to be the guy who says "thank you Ma'am or Sir for your service, even though it sounds cliché, I do mean it" but when there is one red flag on a profile, there are usually more and I have had to ignore people who posed as soldiers because of the red flags on their profile.

Here is a classic example. It sickens me that this happened, but a female soldier contacted me who claimed to be a Sergeant in the Army. I have the greatest respect for our soldiers, but when I went on her profile, there was a huge red flag, and that red flag did not seem to be accompanied with white and blue. She had only one friend. That is so improbable for a female in the Army, it is off-the-chart weird. Since women are vastly outnumbered by men in the Army, I would say it is likely that she could have easily rounded up at least ten fellow soldiers to friend her on F. I would, if for no other reason than we were both decent military people. But unfortunately, this person was not an American soldier, as more red flags became evident. There were only a couple of photos on her profile, and the person who was in one photo might not have been the same as in one of the others. Maybe it was the same person, I couldn't feel sure. Both of these people were females who were in some kind of military function. But were they the same?

So if they weren't the same person, then why wouldn't this other person get tagged? That's a problem. If this female is in the Army, and she has a female friend in the Army that she likes so much to go to this function and take a picture of her fellow soldier and post it on her page, why wouldn't she tag it or at the very minimum, leave a caption as to what's going on or who it was? But that creates a whole other issue,

which is that I cannot get past the idea that if I was a female
(which I am not of course), and I made a female friend in a
situation where everyone else was a male, wouldn't there be
some kind of interesting comraderie?

Unfortunately, the clincher on the profile was the
poverty of information in the "About" section. That was one
red flag too many, and I had to go with the odds on that one. I
guess once in a while I make mistakes, but I've yet to get
anything that contradicts my theories so far.

Sometimes I would get impatient with obvious
scammers and just try to humiliate them outright, as much as
possible. Here is a classic example, with certain things
changed:

> John (who is me):
> want some money?
>
> FS:
> Why ask that
>
> John:
> to see your response
>
> FS:
> You're not giving for me to respond (another classic
example of the lack of English skills that FS usually have)
>
> John:
> huh? try again, that was not readable
>
> FS:
> Do you pay people money just to talk to you
>
> John
> no way. but i like to get the reaction of the facebook
scammers when i say that. most of them can't understand it,
for different reasons.

FS:
Oh
Its seems you've seen more that what you say

John:
Sounds like a foreign expression you are trying to put
into English words
you better get the manager of your boiler room to
translate this stuff for you

FS: It just not okay saying that yo just any body

John:
you're English is so funny!

FS: I think you're reasonable but

John
i meant your English is funny

FS:
You're getting my attention because I'm giving it to you
and its my fault

John:
think about it, it is a sunday afternoon, and you are too
busy to respond. wonder why?
FS:
Who are you?

John:
the person talking to you

FS:
I'm not interested in your cash and you're already
saying your a**out

John

come again? kind of hard to scam someone if you curse them, wouldn't you say little chum?

FS: Its hard to get my response if you continue taking like that

John: it's hard to get your response anyway!

FS: Am not cheap and I have my work I don't beg

John:
so why are you communicating with me if you are in LA and I'm so far away? what's for you to gain?
FS: Don't get you. LA meaning?

John (I was astounded that this scammer did not know the name of the city on "her" own profile, she or he was a terrible scammer. So I decided to make their job a little harder.)
LA stands for an American city called Texas

FS:Ooh there you go huh
This is how you know them huh it's because you fake people take the advantage of ladies on here pissed me off
Its ridiculous

John:
yes i know you have righteous anger, what else makes you mad today?

FS: Its OK have a good day huh... Its kinda irritating when you meet someone on here and you start talking about sex or raking the advantages of each other

John:
but...i thought you were my destiny?

FS: Its all good I'm actually not surprise you talks this way or wanna be taken me for granted I have met peoples like you in the past

(since she seemed to be feeling sexual, I decided to make this male scammer who was not fluent in English feel homosexual. The donkey didn't go for it. Maybe I was right about this FS posing to be a female after all.)

John:
if we kissed, what would it feel like?

FS:Come to think of it. We have not even meet before Lol..

John:
so what? i think it's fun to make out with a new girl or take it further. the newness of the experience is half of the fun

FS:
Well..you are right though but that start from knowing each other well if I'm getting you

John:
no te comprendo

FS: Don't get
no te comprendo meaning?

John
then use translator like you normally do

FS: Oh its now clear
I don't know what you mean
(so he or she thinks it is clear, and doesn't know what I mean?)

John:

you are boring me

FS:
I'm stopping the chat

John
Cool (she is still in the message, I can see.)

looks like you still want to chat?

FS:
It seem you're playing with my head and given you the attention is just a waste of time.

John
that's too bad you are too simple minded to have your head played with

The brutality got worse for the next scammer as I went for the jugular:

Me/John:
hey rossie

FS:
Hello John
How are you

John:
good how are you?

FS:

I'm good
What about you

John:
good what do you do for a living?

FS:
I'm a fashion designer but lay off job
What about you

John:
i work security for facebook. i look for scammers and i
earn my living trying to eat up their time with my entire shift

FS:
Good
Can we have more conversation on hangouts

John:
i'm in the middle of trying to figure out how to get about
300 people to unfriend me today, because i've discovered a
network

FS:
I lost my account on facebook, can you tell me why?

John:
yes i could, but i won't

FS:
Tell me and let me avoid the syntax erro

John:
no because while i make that explanation you will
spend the entire time on another person, and that's not cool

FS:
Alright
I guess you want me to loss this account again and can't talk to you anymore

John:
no i don't want you to loss that account again
the fact of the matter is that you are on facebook to scam somebody out of money, and i hate that

FS:
Scamming
?

John:
yes, your job
(she or he gets quiet, the model who sought me out)

John:
it's what you do for heroin, remember?

FS:
Me?
Heroin?

(he or she tries to play coy. The liar.)

John:
i don't think this is a group chat, or is it?

FS:
You're insulting me here
I must report you

John:
then i guess, it's time to get mad
type the fury into the bar

FS:
You must be stupid

John
sure, if it makes you feel good, my IQ is in the 57
range. and a stupid person has just pegged you

(she disappears)

John:
so how's my friend count now?

(slience)

But then, all is confirmed. I couldn't believe it. I clicked
on her profile name, and I got a message that the profile had
been deleted. The next day, I rechecked to see if I had made
a mistake. I did a search on her name.
    The name that had been on the profile was "Rossie
Miller". No such name now existed, anywhere in the world,
apparently! This is the search results I got back after
searching for her. She had disappeared, this person seeking
publicity in a city that is known for that very thing.

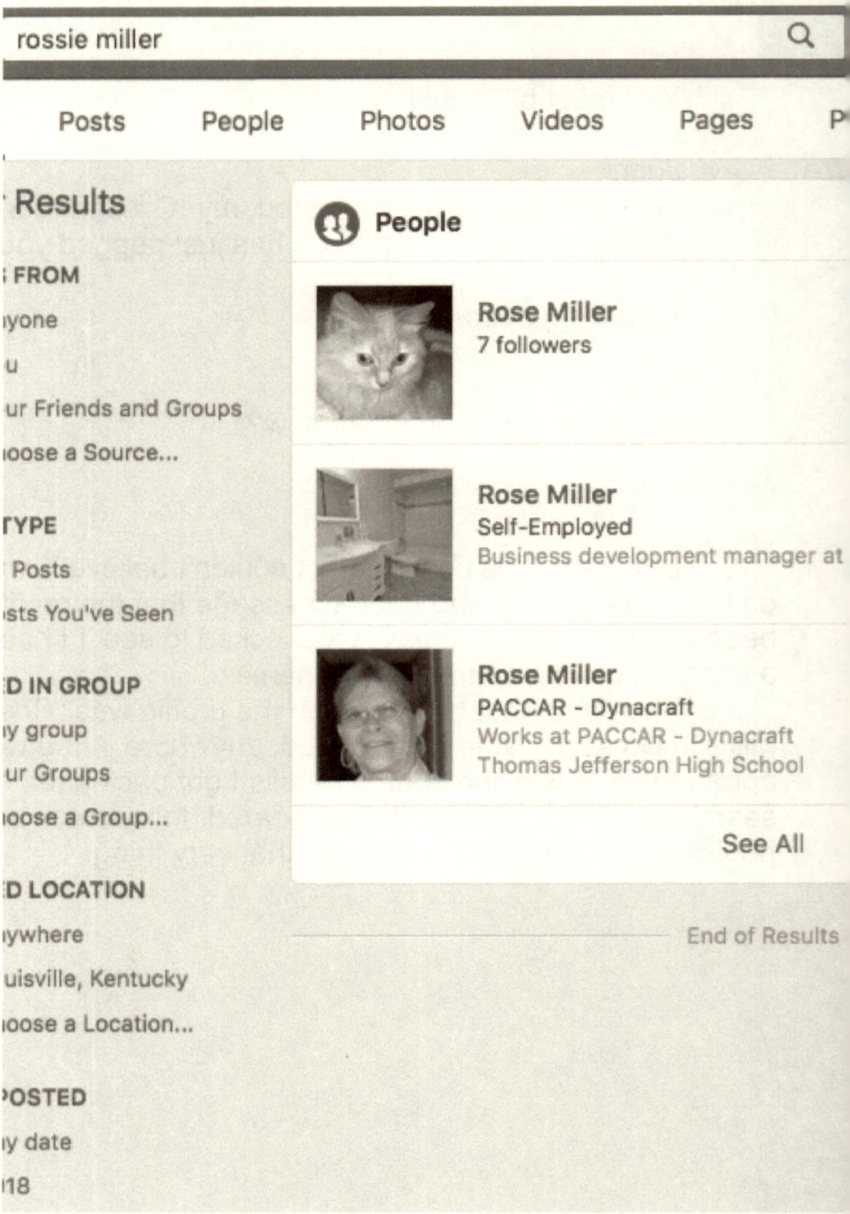

rossie miller

Posts   People   Photos   Videos   Pages   P

Results

People

FROM
yone
u
ur Friends and Groups
oose a Source...

TYPE
Posts
sts You've Seen

D IN GROUP
y group
ur Groups
oose a Group...

D LOCATION
ywhere
uisville, Kentucky
oose a Location...

OSTED
y date
18

Rose Miller
7 followers

Rose Miller
Self-Employed
Business development manager at

Rose Miller
PACCAR - Dynacraft
Works at PACCAR - Dynacraft
Thomas Jefferson High School

See All

End of Results

Another thing about the name "Rossie" is that it is not a normal spelling, and I feel convinced that it is a misspelling. In my experience, if I met a woman named something similar, it would be more likely to be "Rosie". I would not be too shocked if I met a woman named "Ross", but "Rossie"? That name sounds to me to be of foreign origin, or not spelled correctly. Either way, we have a FS. **A normal person would never misspell their own first name**.

Never. It is the first name we learn to write and is likely written roughly as much as we write the word "the". It's more like a reflex, and it will not fail. Unless of course, you are living in Bulgaria and need money for crack right away. That is usually the time you cannot remember your own name. And a person in Bulgaria is not likely to come to America and have coffee with me for 30 minutes. I'm not saying it's impossible, but I'd probably be more likely to get that date if the woman was at least American. I have nothing against Bulgarian women. If one was nice, fluent in English, and wanted to date, it could happen. But not through F.

Since the gender bending seems to be a problem for most FS, that must be where the band aid was I needed to hit. Most men are not gay, statistically. That's when I realized how to twist their arms for maximum pain. They would have to tell me sexual things that only a woman would know, and would have to read my stuff. And if they lost interest, I'd have to threaten to withhold the money I wasn't going to give them in the first place. This brings up another point.

Because most FS are not always in America or in English-speaking lands, they make mistakes when it comes to the normal names for a woman or man. Without fail, if I see a woman with a man's name on it, it is an FS, and I have yet to find exception. That is another easy superficial way to tell right away who NOT to send money to. The other people NOT to send money to, are in my opinion, **everyone else**, internet, live or bleeding to death.

The reason why I am such a cruel and merciless individual is, believe it or not, to help people! Society's problems are not about money. God can give any individual the resources they might need in any situation. But if the individual turns their back on God, and looks for a handout, the Man Upstairs might be disappointed, having been denied the opportunity to start a relationship with a great person. Was that too much to ask in the first place?

I hate to be the messenger that gets killed because of the message, but apparently so. FS are in such a desperate state and without any moral heading that they turn to the methods of the devil, a vile creature that I so despise, his is the only proper name I refuse to capitalize. Maybe that's why I am self-published…

Time-tested ethics of publishers aside, vast as they are in the Big Apple, FS make a great number of mistakes on their profiles that scream "scam". And if I detect a "scam" then I hate to say "scram". When I say scram, that means they close out my message, despite the fact that I'm about to take down the aisle another up and coming actress who doesn't know one of the largest cities in the world that she works in. The inevitable result is they can more quickly move on to the next sucker.

But should I protect the world from itself? What did the world do for me? As I have written in my other books I have self-published, especially **Schizoid: The Native Immigrant** (I hang my head low for the shame of my plug!), the answer is that the world in repeated methods and in unpredictable ways wanted me dead or at least in pain. So I was I to survive? It's easy. I went to God, and found the answer. He told me to be a hero. I had the guts, the know how, and the time. I went for it, and if society puts me back on the top of their public enemy list again, I'll still find a way to frustrate a scammer.

I found it to be a healthy and refreshing way to get my anger out. Women wouldn't date me, despite the large checks I offered them. Guys did not want to hang out, lest they get infected with the Bible. I lived in the shadows, alone. Sometimes I died in a private way, or wanted to. The knife seemed to have a magnetic gravitation to my throat. I wanted to make the cut, but then I realized that if I made that fatal mistake, that a scammer was getting the opportunity to get free money. So it kept me going, and then, the idea for this book came along, and things got better. More copies moved, my radio show came along, and some of the small improvements I had been making on a daily basis began to pay off. It wasn't easy. But the value of the things I did were immense, and I chronicled everything in my last book (here I go again, I should have been an outlet the way I plug!) **Fat Nobody Becomes Athletic Genius**!

My hilarious Carson appearance notwithstanding, names are apparently too difficult for the average FS to understand. I guess they could have used certain resources that most English-speaking people know about, but if I mention that right now, this game will get harder on me. For the moment, I think I'll reserve that particular advantage for our team. But that is not nearly the only problem they have.

Let me bring up a few grammatical errors, and demonstrate how they are tell-tale signs of FS.

This is an excerpt of the "Rossie" chat:

FS:
I'm a fashion designer but <u>lay off job</u>
What about you

John:
i work security for facebook. i look for scammers and i earn my living trying to eat up their time with my entire shift

FS:
Good
Can we <u>have more conversation</u> on hangouts

When I inspect the two grammatical errors in combination, I can nearly hear the accent as though it was the oncoming siren of an ambulance. I won't give away too much just in case the slime balls get a copy of this book, but of course, they would have to learn to read it! I have a feeling my average number of stars might fall a bit after they leave their review. That's ok because there are other reasons that they are not likely to read this book, which is mainly that it is unavailable in countries that have the most scammers. This book won't come out anywhere in Africa, which includes the largest country in that continent by land, Sudan, and the wealthiest country over there, which is South Africa, but I wouldn't call South Africa "wealthy". The last news blip I saw about that country depicted footage of people carrying around jugs of water. I don't think those people are too worried about an American self-published lunatic, unless of course things have changed.

Back to the grammar, I'll dig into it a bit. The first problem is "lay off job". Non-English speakers struggle with certain verbal situations that are natural for us. That FS, most likely was European, because I've been around some ex-patriots from Russian, or other ex-Soviet countries and it is the kind of mistake they make. An American would say "I got laid off". Nobody in any English-speaking country would say "I'm a fashion designer but lay off job." It sounds like some kind of translator robot.

A good example of this occurs in the Sean Connery movie from 1990 "The Russia House". Connery plays a Brit, but Michelle Pfeffier, an American actress, does an outstanding Russian in her role. It correlates with the type of accent that certain people usually have and the type of grammatical mistakes that they make, and those people come from countries with Cyrillic alphabets, which were part of the USSR back in the day.

This small part of the conversation had other grammatical errors too. Most Americans would not say "I'm a fashion designer but I got laid off." Americans don't think like that. Americans are a fluid, industrious and intelligent people who once in a while for a lot of reasons, change careers. It's a different mind set than in Europe and countries that used to be part of communist Russia. Those people usually developed a career path, many times it was not what a person wanted to do, but they stayed with it because that's just the way it works over there. If a person was a fashion designer, they went to

40

school for it, worked in it all of their life and never changed careers. Why exactly other countries operate that way, I don't know but I suspect that in economic environments that are marginal, people are too close to the gutter to take risks.

This FS might have attempted to read a magazine or saw something on TV one time and was able to get the jist of what was going on. This FS has no understanding of how the American mindset works in a real career field. But also, I have a theory which is that most FS don't know how ANY career works because their only career is illegal and immoral, which is to beg and manipulate strangers for money. And when they are not behind a computer, what else that happens is far less marginal and is overtly wrong. What else I am referring to, are things I've already mentioned; drugs, prostitution, guns, murder, evading the law, extortion, scams and schemes a plenty. A FS doesn't know anything about a real career because they have not worked one. Sometimes, when they are young, they might have had a job stacking bricks in the heat, selling trinkets to tourists, or maybe even worked up to a part-time cashier position. Unfortunately, those days for the FS have faded more quickly than the spelling of the name that is not theirs.

I can speak plainly about myself because over my years, I have worked between 50-60 jobs. I have flipped burgers, spot welded in a factory, collected negative debt that was owed on trailers, sold pre-need cemetery plots, all of which flowed into the natural career paths of claims adjusting, delivering pizza and cutting grass. Of course, I was after all, a musician. This is how it goes in America: we can't be contained! We're too smart to sit around, worry and cry for a career that won't happen. We move on to the next thing if it fails.

But the problems do not end there. How many fashion designers get laid off? My guess is that there are people that design clothes FOR fashion designers, but a fashion designer, as I understood it, from the days when I was on Saville Row, was not the type of career that someone worked in a 9-5 operation with a punchcard. I could be wrong, but I thought those types worked to create their own designs and build a brand label. And if the career path of being a "fashion designer" led to someone being "lay off job", what are the odds that I would be on the other end of their message, since that entire number of workers in that field is measured in Angstrums to begin with? It makes a baccarat table look like a government bond, in comparison. Forget it, it won't happen.

An obvious mistake is also the absence of question marks. Even on text and M, most Americans will include a question mark because if we need to know something right now, it is natural for us to go ahead and add it. In that manner, the person receiving the message is aware that we want or need an answer. Many foreign languages, even when written do not use question marks. An example is Japanese. A speaker of Japanese waits until the end of a sentence to hear "ka". If the Japanese speaker hears it, he or she knows it is a question, but there are many other cues as well. But the "ka" makes it a certainty that the questioner, is at the moment, uncertain. The receiver knows a question has been posed to him or her. The absence of a question mark is problematic.

This goes into a deeper aspect of the American psyche. The reason we include question marks in txts and M most of the time is because as I mentioned we need to know something right now. But this is different than the kind of urgency that the rest of the world experiences. The rest of the world works a maximum of 30 hours per week during the rush, is disinterested in the needs of customers, and has a disengaged and skeptical view of their environment. The reason that an American makes sure to use a question mark is not because they need the information now: they needed it last week! But did they? Likely not. But in America, people have a tendency to turn on a dime and view loyalty as something owed only to God. Even the lowly cashier in America is well-aware of the cheetah-like acceleration and agility of the consumer or businesses in America. And this is an advantage we have in identifying the FS, which is the ability to spot deception because of their utter laziness to make a keystoke that REQUIRES the SHIFT key with it. It makes me wonder about exactly how calorie-deprived they actually are, to miss out on a critical aspect of their fraud.

This speaks to the comparative pace, enthusiasm, and fearless quest for excellence and prosperity of an American. A FS does not understand that because they seldomly research American culture. They do not understand how our use of English is different than what they were taught (which normally comes from England) and complete fluency is difficult for the most learned of scholars. A heroin addict with a computer will never have the drive and "ummph!" (as we call it over here) to succeed at anything, especially learning to write in a foreign language even though their habit depends upon it. The basic skills a FS developed in English only came because of being in a school system that started them on English in kindergarden, but by the time high school arrived, most of them are in the midst of departure from book learning. And in many cases, that departure was notably sooner. That is a sad reality of places that are not considered territories of industrialized nations. Scholarship rarely exists for the people on the wrong side of the tracks, even over in the land of the free.

The other part of that phrase is "can we have more conversation..." That is so awkward to see written in a chat or M. I'm from the south, and if I wanted someone to move to another website or chatroom to talk, I wouldn't say it anything like that. Since my goal is to help English-speakers recognize what scammers say, I believe that wording stands alone without further explanation. It is the type of sentence structure and awkwardness a foreigner has when they communicate in English with only a primitive command of certain types of things. I won't go into it deeper. The novice scammer might read this part, which is a powerful tool to put the smackdown on criminals.

If an English speaker has read this far into this book, they can be certain to have enough of the language to know the basic problems that plague such a simple statement. It is the kind of distorted weirdness that I **want** to hear in real life if I try to pick up a woman, like an added bonus for the exotic excitement that doesn't require an expensive flight. It motivates me a little more and makes me want to get her digits for a date than the girl from Illinois, for some reason. Also what is important to note that the reason a foreigner makes a mistake like that is because they are trying to translate word for word the natural way that the rules of their native language dictate.

As my Spanish teacher taught me, and also as I have learned independently, you must speak "good Spanish for good Spanish", which means that you can't just slum around in a foreign language and expect to be understood. But if all you can do is be understood, then it will be plain as day to a native that you did not start on their language. Which is not going to be a problem for people with honest intentions who work REAL jobs that pay LEGAL money.

As I mentioned this resource will only work for a temporary time. If it helps some people for a while that is a good thing. I personally believe that every time I spend an hour distracting FS, is money in the bank of Americans. There are no statistics on this subject, but I think that once in a while I save somebody a house or the equivalent. All I needed to save was one for my whole career, but I'll do it a Lincoln at a time if necessary. That's because I'm called to do this thing, and I love it. The wind is at my back. My suggestion the next time life gets choppy, is to find someone with a weird name and go to town on them! Waste their time! Make them think you are about to give them money, and as the Great Buckwheat Zydeco said, when you stall the FS, "Take your time, son!" Buck was the man.

But on bad days, the brutality continued:

FS (making intitial contact with me, the first red flag)
Hello

John
hi

FS:
Good morning (morning? It was nearly midnight or later when
we started. Red flag #2)
John
what up

FS:
Cool dear and you

John
cool dear

FS:
Ok that is good

John
quiet! (I was trying to txt with a real person and this scammer
was annoying with the repeated messages)

FS:
So where do you from

John
quiet!

FS:
Your country

John
oh good. which part?

FS:
Your home town

John
this requires researching the name of a foreign city right now,
unfortunately
so get out google maps, and get started, i'll wait

bye

you wouldn't even name a scottish city>

FS:
(gives phone number) number

John
somethings amiss as they say
I continue:
do you seriously think i'm going to call you:?

FS:
Yes

John
i mean do you think that?
i would say you might think about doing something other than
scamming people

FS:
On whatsapp

John
you aren't much of a scammer (this is how dumb they are,
they don't know enough English to understand that I'm
insulting the crap out of her. It gets worse too.)

FS:
Am not

John
yes i agree that you suck at scamming money from people
that's because you suck at everything

FS:
No

John
yes becaue that's why you scam people.

you have no career and you inject heroin
and you just aren't intelligent in any way.

you're a moron

yes?

say something

FS:
Am not a scammer

John
turd
yes i would agree that you cannot scam, but no i disagree that
you are not a scammer

FS:
It your choice

John
you can't even read

FS:
I can read
Here is not a class room (usually scammers get impatient
during a text that goes longer than ten or so lines)

John
you need a classroom, believe me! and also, **you need
class**.

(she disappears, her profile is gone, still I try again)
go ahead and tell me about the 7.6 million dollars i won

<u>Sometimes things they say are downright hilarious:</u>

FS:
Hi

John
Hi

FS:
Am Fine And You

John
you work for the Astros? (her profile said that she worked for the Astros of Houston. The scammers can't even style the team name correctly.)

FS:
Where Are You From

(classic scammer dialogue, to ignore questions in order to move a mark into a position where they can get money)

John
did you STOP working for the Astros or something?

FS:
Yes

John
so you work for the cubs now, you said? (she has no idea what's going on at this point)

FS:
Am Doing Make-up Now

48

John
oh ok <u>you do the **make up*** for the cubs</u>.

(it's astounding how little English scammers know. I could feel
sorry for them, but I just don't. I continue with this bizarre
dialogue.)

John (again)
i think that's why they did so well in the world series a few
years back, it was because of the eyeliner

FS:
Yes (she couldn't understand a word of it, obviously)

John
You should stick to make up
Or I guess make up should stick to you?

<u>More evidence of the utter incompetence of the FS:</u>

FS (they make first contact)
Im here

John
Hi

FS:
My dear are you marrid

John
marred? no i have no mars on the surface of this table

FS:
Okay but why at your age ?

John
huh?

i don't know the table surface is smooth at my age

----Profile Not Found----

<u>Here is another outdated derelict, with the ancient lottery angle (my goal here was just to make him type meaningless crap for a while) (he makes first contact):</u>

Hello there how are you doing? My name is FS:. I am a legal representative of the Floyd Mayweather Jr Foundation and T.M.T THE MONEY TEAM . I just wanted to urgently notify you that your Facebook account was recently raffled up in the T.M.T The Money Team balloting system in which you were selected as the lucky grand prize winner in our third category draw of $7,500,000 (7.5) million dollars and a brand new 2018 Mercedes-Benz (MODEL: GLE) on the behalf of Floyd Mayweather.

John
Hi (I am feeling bad for Floyd Mayweather at this point, for the FS to be using his name like that. Floyd should beat the crap out this FS. I feel confident he could do it too!)

FS:
Do you want to officailly claim your certified winnings today sir?

John
how much?

FS:
Hello there how are you doing? My name is FS:. I am a legal representative of the Floyd Mayweather Jr Foundation and T.M.T THE MONEY TEAM . I just wanted to urgently notify you that your Facebook account was recently raffled up in the T.M.T The Money Team balloting system in which you were selected as the lucky grand prize winner in our third category

draw of $7,500,000 (7.5) million dollars and a brand new 2018 Mercedes-Benz (MODEL: GLE) on the behalf of Floyd Mayweather.

John
how much?

FS:
7.5 million and your brand new 2018 Mercedes Benz

John
how much is it?

FS:
First of all for security purposes I will be providing you with a seven digit prize number wich should be kept strictly confidential and you should use this prize number whenever someone from this or any other organization's call you in regards to your certified winnings, this is for your own security is this understood?

John
ok go ahead with the seven digit prize number

FS:
Now your seven digit prize number is *3323069* always bear your prize number in mind for further use.

John
339798987 was it? (I was mocking the subhuman.)

FS:
3323069is
Please provide the required information needed for claiming and delivery
FULL NAME
•FULL ADDRESS

•PHONE NUMBER these are the only information we require from our claimers in getting prize claimed.

John
my name is FS:, my address is Africa and my phone number is 3323069

FS:
Ok

(profile disappears)

This one turned out to be comic GOLD:

FS (making first contact as usual):
hello
how are you doing

FS:
hello
how are you doing
my name is FS: my second name is Alex am from Nashville
Nice to meet you

(my "second name" is Alex? That has scammer written all over it, for a lot of reasons.)

John
me too, what hospital were you born there?

FS:
I buy in USA

(what prompted her to respond like that? She was probably overloaded with other scamjobs.)

John
you bought a hospital? (this starts to get funnier)

52

FS:
Nope
my mother born me in home

John
she "born" you in home?

FS:
yes
she don't go to the hospital she born me in home

John
what city in america?

FS:
am in Tennessee

John
Tennessee's a nice city

FS:
thank you
where are you from

John
you're welcome, <u>you did a good job creating Tennessee</u>. (she
did, after all, thank me for admiring her apparent creation of
the state of Tennessee. But whether Tennessee is a city or
state, God knows and I know, He was the Creator of it. This
scammer can't read.)
John
how long did it take you to build the <u>city</u> of tennessee?

FS:

well am not working at the moment , i am working with a
company before and the manager was trying to raped me so i
run away from him and he his in jail now.

(she can't apparently, understand any of what I am saying at
this point.)

John
so did you work for the construction company that built the city
of tennessee?

FS:
am working with Walmart before

John
oh so i understand now. <u>Walmart built the city of Tennessee</u>!

John (she's done so I finish her off. Her boss came over and
told her to move on probably.)
ok here it is in wikipedia. you were right. walmart built the city
of tennessee in 1993

**<u>Another FS chat. This one has on her profile that she
lives in Cebu City. I tend to think her profile was more
accurate than her dialogue. In fact, I guarantee it. Keep in
mind that the Eagles had just won the Superbowl that
year, which was 2018, against Tom Brady and The
unstoppable Patriots, with their 5 recent championships.
The FS, knows nothing about any of this.</u>**

FS makes first contact
Hi

FS
ok
when you online john

FS

Halo

John
Hi

FS
nice to meet you john? im from phil?
John
i guess you all were happy this year

FS
thanks you john why happy this year?

John
hmmmm, i thought there was something interesting that
happened to phil this year, maybe i could be wrong

FS
what happened this year in phil? why wrong?

John
i was thinking about government, or film, or maybe transit?
(she must live in a cave)

FS
ah so you like to meet me in my place your welcome for me?
im single no bf?

John
i was wondering about phil, if something happened or not

FS
yeah you try here? if you want me you stay with me?

John
it seemed like i saw something in the news about
pennsylvania, am i wrong?

FS
ah ok you dont like to come in phil

John
it sounds gay what you wrote (she can't understand why that
would be a gay joke)(no offense to gays)

FS
what?
what are you looking here in senoir dating?

John
i was wondering what event could have happened this year
regarding phil?

FS
ah so you dont like to come in phil?
John
it seems like this event was known by a lot of people, but i'm
not sure

FS
ok
for me im here in seniuor dating to found relationship?

John
hmmmm, i wonder if anybody knows what happened in
philadelphia this year?
maybe somebody knows at a local "SPORTS BAR"

FS
im sory im a good woman? i till you? im frank woman ? for me
im still virgin untill now? i reserve my virginity?

John
wait i know, it was basketball?

FS

what basketble?

John
my bad it was the Olympics

FS
what are you saying?

John
i thought i just said it?

FS
what is said about ?

John
Yawn

FS
what?

(I usually write yawn when I'm ready to move on to the next FS, to signal myself that it's over.)

Another classic hallmark of the FS is that they never go to school or work careers, so it's easy to puzzle them. They know virtually nothing about anything. Here is an example:

FS
How are you?

John
good how are you?

FS
I'm fine
Nice too meet you

John
nice two meet you to

FS
Tell me more about you

John
i do a lot of stuff. what is your career?

FS
Am a nurse
What's your career

John
i'm a zookeeper
jk

FS
Ok

John
so which picture is yours? (two of the pictures on the profile
did not match. One was clearly from the 1970s or 80s. The
other looked way more current.)

FS
That's my mom pics on the display pics

John
i see the family resemblance

FS
Thanks

John
i would not put my mother's face on my profile, but i could be
weird

FS
Lol

John
so you are a nurse in sc with your mom's picture on your
profile?

FS
Yes

John
i had a question about the human body since you are a nurse.
could you help me?

FS
Ok

John
so what is more important for daily functioning, dopamine or
seratonin?
Seen by FS at 11:04pm

John
any luck on the neurotransmitter deal?

(dead silence from the nurse)

**<u>Here's another FS who can't figure out what I might be
referring to, which is the television show Miami Vice with
Don Johnson, which was incredibly popular in the 1980s.
Everyone in America knows about it. Except for this
Florida Miami resident:</u>**

FS initiates with a wave, then I answer:
what is going on?

FS
Nothing much

You ?

John
nothing. where are you located

FS
Florida Miami
You?

John
interesting
it made me think of a tv show. how about you?

FS
Don't understand that

(this is the way they behave on M, which is they sense that
you know something they do not know, and they get a little
defensive. They always respond by going on the offensive, or
otherwise try to distract me by acting like they are interested,
which for most men works. But not a guy who is set on
destroying the FS.)

FS continues:
Where are you from too?

John
hmmm was there a tv show in florida or something?

FS
Yes there is a lot of tv shows over here (unnatural usage of a
verb)

John
hmm i wonder if there was a tv show in miami or something?

FS
There is

John
there is or there was?

(goes dead)

<u>Other obvious signs of the FS:</u>

1. Women who are scantily clad in their profile picture or pictures in their profile.

2. Women **not** from America.

3. Women who make first contact.

4. Women who friend me that I've never met in real life.

5. Men who I've never met in real life.

6. Women who have less than around 100 friends.

7. Women who have very few posts other than a couple of pictures.

8. Women with only a couple of pictures of themselves in their "Photos".

9. In the "About" section, most of the information is blank, or doesn't match up with what is known about that information.

10. Many scammers use American last names for first names. An example might be Smith Jane. F always styles American names the correct way.

11. Many FS use words that aren't really names, like "Lovely Grace". I've never met anyone named

"Lovely" in my life, and I doubt that there's an American mom that would do that to her child. But if it was true, maybe that's why Lovely got so jacked up to become a FS in the first place!

12. An FS knows nothing about basic American culture.

13. Some FS work the sex angle and send porn right away. I've wondered where they get these pictures, the Africans, of blond-haired Caucasian women who are so flawless. I guess necessity is the mother of invention.

14. The "Friends" of the FS, which are few in number, have foreign names.

15. The "Timeline" is a dead giveaway, which has almost nothing there, and after only a small number of posts, has a white block that reads "Posts from ______(year of birth)___" and nothing below it.

16. Sometimes they repeat a first or last name for their whole name: Arlena Arlena. Another example of how lazy and careless they usually are.

17. The town where they claim to live in America doesn't exist or is a small bedroom community that emerged within the last decade. They usually claim it as their hometown.

18. There is usually no information that is directly above their name in M or on their profile. They assume that nobody notices, but I notice right away, and that is usually indicative of the FS.

19. Another mistake they make is to look up the name of a state and call their location that city, for example Massachusetts City, Massachusetts.

20. If you ask them about a hit song, a rock band that was popular in America, TV shows, movies, etc. they can't answer any questions about it.

21. They become defensive when they can't answer your questions about everyday things.

22. Their profession is "self-employed" and they are female. A self-employed person in America would, without exception, put their business on F. And it could be verified outside of F.

23. Usually a female with a first name for a last name is in the FS.

Take a look at this screenshot of a so-called "friend":

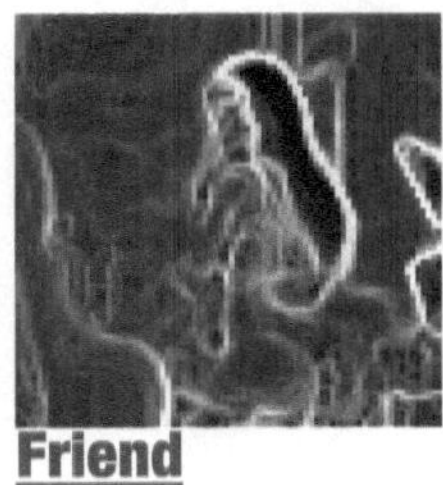

Friend

Friends

Ashley M*&^*&^*
University of Oxford

I guess she majored in pole dancing at Oxford? Looks like she probably made the Dean's List again… Here's another classic:

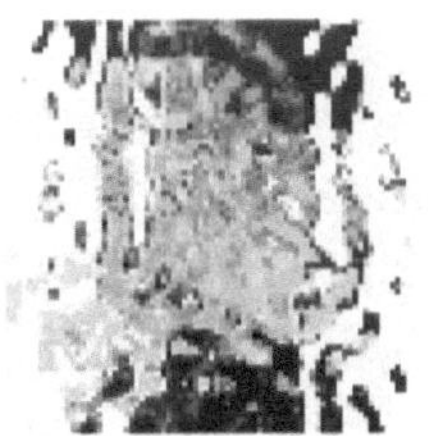

Jenny K
Infantry Officer at U.S Soldiers

She must have been in the conjugal unit. They were known
for taking many men through psychological warfare. She
definitely was not in the unit that specializes in the English
language: "Infantry Officer at U.S Soldiers".

She would have had my whole bank account, except
that "Infantry Officer" is kind of a contradiction in terms. Most
officers in the Army are and were extremely capable soldiers,
but as they rise through the ranks via hard work, move away
from the front lines where the "Infantry" are located, in order to
specialize, which makes them more effective.

The term "U.S Soldiers" is also the type of generic
intermediate fluency that would make sense to a foreigner, but
as usual, sounds weird or awkward to an American. As much
as I would love to help them improve upon the skills they
should have learned during the days when they were skipping
school in order to learn to steal, there is another problem.
Look at the missing period after "S" in "U.S". It's probably not
a mistake an American would make. We learn how to
abbreviate for the U.S.A. or U.S. early on. Unless of course
my career path was in scamming, in which the only thing I
knew was learning a pre-arranged script in order to
manipulate someone.

Here's another different FS mistake that always cracks me up:

Intro

- Works at Kuban State University
- Lives in Raleigh, North Carolina

Since I'd never heard of "Kuban State University", I had
to look it up. It's in southern Russia near the Black Sea. I
guess she doesn't mind the commute from Raleigh. Probably
there is not much traffic across the Atlantic. But everybody
has a rush hour, I guess. Maybe she has a shortcut, like

going over the North Pole or something. I wonder what radio stations come in? (Radio stations cannot be tuned in that far away). She'll need an oil change every day!

This one stands on its own as comedy:

Елена Тимченко
Corpus Christi, Texas

I'm not saying it's impossible that she is from Texas, but usually women from that area are named Tammy Sue. Couple the photo of the model with the Cyrillic alphabetic name, make it likely we have a member of the official FS.

Another FS has determined that I'm a complete moron:

Lilly Gold
California, Missouri

Was there the possibility that there was a town in Missouri called "California"? Suprisingly enough, there is a California in Missouri. This small town has a population of 4,200+ and is dead-center in the state, probably two hours' drive from the Arch. Again, to find someone from this town who is a model was exciting because there would be less competition from other guys in the town. If I were to continue this kind of fortune, I'd be stupid to not buy a scratch-off.

In this case, I struck gold twice:

Intro

- o   Lives in California, Missouri
- o   From California, Maryland

I guess we have somebody who went from California to California, and never got west of Nevada! But there is a California, Maryland too! Wikipedia says that it was named after the state. Maybe next time, they'll name it after the altruistic writer who saves the public from the FS. Or, Bukowski works too… He wasn't into F too much though.

Here's a woman who claims to be a "lady guard" in Cebu City, Philippines. (I'm starting to become more familiar with Phillippine geography than with American small towns, especially if they are named after states, apparently! I wondered if there was a state named "Cebu"?)

I wondered if the "lady guarding" business was in decline? This beautiful blonde in the Phillipines was hitchhiking. It appears that she picked a bad time to stick out her thumb. She could have ordered a Lyft. She could have sold her designer purse and heels. Maybe Lyft would hire her, but she'd have to make the leap of faith. Also interesting is:

Intro

- lady guard at Best Emporium, Pagadian City
- Self-Employed
- Lives in Pagadian, Pagadian, Philippines
- From Camanga, Zamboanga Del Sur, Philippines

Here's her real photo:

So this woman has dyed her hair, is self-employed while working as a "lady guard" and has professional pictures taken of her from the rear while hitchhiking on a desolate street?   It all seems logical to me…

Here we have a pair of "self-employed" twins with a man's name (who might make a good pair of lady guards should they be able to thumb a ride to the mall). I guess they would have numerical superiority in matters of security. James M. here does look pretty vicious. They should put him (or her? Or them?) into the infantry as an officer:

James M
Works at Self-Employed

Here's a "Michelle Brown" from "Qobu". This one is particularly funny to me because my friend set me up with a girl when I was in the eighth grade who went by the alias of "Michelle Brown". I often wonder how many Browns, Smiths and Millers there were on F? This one in my opinion was more likely to know Елена Тимченко.

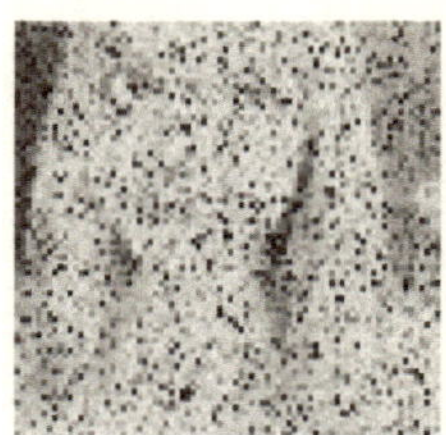

Michelle Brown

Qobu, Abşeron, Azerbaijan

I did a search. The screen filled with just "Michelle Brown"s. And if there are more Michelle Browns than there are actual Michelle Browns, then the number of total people with the surname of Brown is astronomical. I wonder if sometimes employees of F just highlight a bunch of Browns and delete them, for the heck of it? The amount of space needed to accommodate the empty profiles of "Michelle Browns" is probably proportional to the commute across the Atlantic.

Here's another occurrence of striking gold. I just got spotted by a talent agent! In Lebanon (enthusiasm wanes…). But, it could still work. Do they have a Lebo-wood over there or something? I guess she made good connections in the Lebanese entertainment industry during her time at the University of South Alabama. Maybe she was in the marching band?

68

Intro

- Works at (*&(*&(Talent Agency
- Studied at The University of South Alabama
- Lives in Sidon, Lebanon

<u>Name Anomolies:</u>

Here's a woman who has a first name that I am not too crazy about, heir apparent to the bottled water company:

Adolph Evian
Mark as Spam
Request removed.

He or she does not yet have a name:

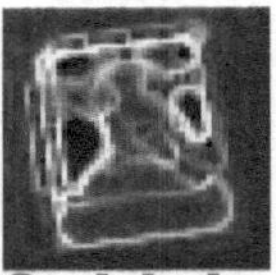

Curlyhair
Mark as Spam
Request removed.

Here's a guy named Brooke, apparently Hispanic by last name, who enjoys listening to the radio during an oceanic rush hour:

Brooke Trujillo

Here's an Asian woman with a Cyrillic name who is friends with Dawn Smith (?):

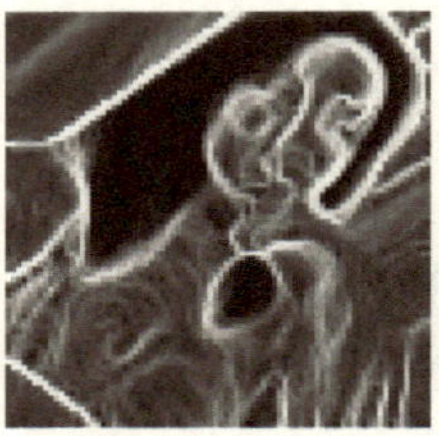

Мария Горюнова

Dawn Smith and 6 other mutual friends

This scammer hardly looks old enough to drive. At least she spends her time wisely by falling in love with a guy that can't speak her language on the other side of the world. As Adam Carolla used to say on Loveline, "Perfectly normal, perfectly legal.":

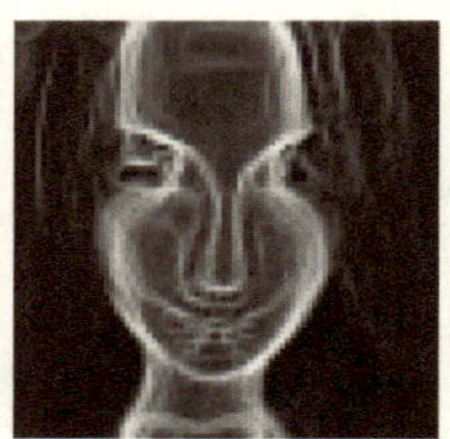

Елена Смирнова

Finally my dreams came true when I had the opportunity to date a stuffed animal:

(name removed)
Boss at Self-Employed

This three year old operates a computer better than she can write. Everyone's got priorities, I guess:

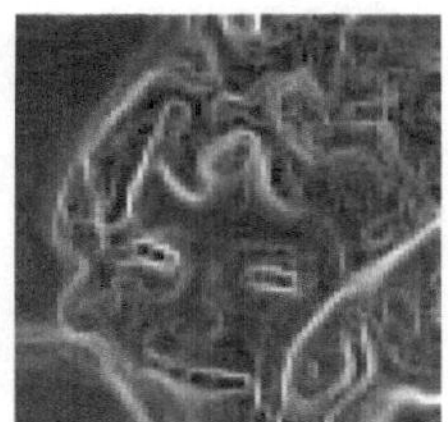

Aillision R*******

Here's a picture of a woman who calls herself "Rose Jack". I can't accuse her of being in the FS, but the information sure is marginal. The profile picture is the only one I could show in my book because the rest are too suggestive. The rest of her profile is littered with red flags. The first one is the obvious first name as a last name, which with few exceptions, lead back to the FS.

She hails from Van, Turkey. That is the only information she gives, other than a few posts, all of which are scantily clad pictures. Here is one of her posts: "Say your mind about me". What nagged me the most was probably that she was underage and had not even reached the still-young birthday of 18 before she joined the FS. If she had made such a transition some years back, one could only imagine what kind of schemes this person was conducting in real life.

Then I thought back on my own information. These were just pictures. The person operating this profile was probably not even a woman. They were part of a larger syndicate of FS who put out volumes of profiles, using the images of women. I wondered how many of these profiles were female at all?

I had to consider the possibility that the answer was none. The Bible uses the word "prostitute" in conjunction with the word for "pornography" in the Greek. Essentially this woman was by Biblical definition a prostitute, if God had folded everyone who sells sexually stimulating images for profit.

The bizarre convos continued with some more of the FS, who usually claim to be American. The truth lies in the content of the communication:

FS (first contact):
How are you?

John
good u?

FS:
Same here

John
where do you live?

FS:
I'm from Ohio, but I stay in Houston Texas now
And you?

John
that's not what your profile says
where is "Ohio City"?
I live in Kentucky City. I used to live in Indiana City.

FS:
Wellington
Good

John
I'm thinking of moving to either Connecticut City, or maybe
Idaho City

FS:
Why?

John
it was between that and Kansas City. As you know, there is
no such place as Kansas City

FS:
Sure dear
You single or married?
(the FS always tries to make it all about romance as quickly as
possible.)

John
Minnesota City is nice in the winter. I like to summer in
Ecuador

FS:
Yeah
You single or married?

John
i forgot

FS:

Forgot?

John
Yes

FS:
Forgot what?

John
scroll up if you've lost track

FS:
Ok
What do you for living?

John
bicycle messenger

FS:
Is that a job

John
didn't you see quicksilver? (she has no idea about the Kevin
Bacon movie, as usual.)

FS:
Please say reasonable something   ok

John
reasonable something ok
i just did what you asked, didn't i?

FS:
Ok
Do you stay alone? And why do you decide to be single?

John

74

what are you, a free psychologist or something?

(Line goes dead.)

<u>I continue on to the next FS, who wants to hit me up right away:</u>

FS, first contact, a woman with a first name for a last name:
Hello

John
sup?

FS:
How are you doing

John
Aight

FS:
Where are you from

John
how do you define it?

FS:
Where do you live

John
Tierre Del Fuego

<u>For some reason, she stopped talking to me. Does she hate where I live? I always thought living in the land of fire was a good location since Antarctica was close…</u>

<u>The next one was into polyandry. And she was proud of it too!</u>

FS hits me up first:
Hello

John
Hi

FS:
How are you
I'm Cole Lola from Pennsylvania USA

FS:
Hello

John
sure you are

FS:
Tell me about yourself

John
like what?

FS:
Name, country, job and family

John
My name is Edward Lee Roth, from the Netherlands, my job is
a ditch digger, and my family is a whole other story

FS:
Good
So how is life in Netherlands
I'm presently in west Africa for masters program which I just
finished last month
I have never been to Netherlands before (unfortunately, being
on social media and living in Africa generally equates to
scammer.)

John
me neither

FS:
Why you
Don't you stay in Netherlands
?

John
yes i mean no

FS:
Ok
Where do you stay in Netherlands
I do watch football and I like Van Persie from Netherlands

John
336 Elm Street, next to Amstel brewery

FS:
Wow
A popular place

John
i got it for a song.

FS:
One day I will be there
Song?

John
it's an American expression, you wouldn't understand.
(she doesn't get why I said that, an American expression for a
cheap price.)

FS:
And are you an American?

John
Nah

FS:
OK
That's good
Can you tell me how many kids you have

John
it's good that I'm not American? nobody can control where
they are born, right?

FS:
I don't mean that. You can always be a citizen of America if
you you like
There are many ways of being a citizen of America

John
is that right? well, sorry i don't switch. i was born in nijemen,
and I'm not leaving!

FS:
Ok

John
what kind of reaction is that?
ok?

FS:
Its always good to stick to a place
And also good to travel wide
One of my hubby is to travel
(nice English skills, very marginal, which I exploit as the convo
continues.)

John
that's why i carry glue to put on my pants, and a crowbar

FS:
That's what you want

John
so one of your husbands is to travel?

FS:
But will you take me round Netherlands if I come?

John
i guess the other husbands DON'T travel?

FS:
I don't have a husband yet
I mean what I like is to travel
Hubbie

John
you said one of your husbands likes to travel, so which
husband does the traveling of all of your husbands?

FS:
I'm single

John
so i guess ALL of your husbands have travelled!
(she doesn't get my jokes, not enough fluency. I'm deadpan
anyway!)

FS:
No husband yet
I'm single
I'm taking of hubbies not husband

John
yes i know you feel that way when your husbands are on the
road

FS:
What do you mean
Don't you understand words?

John
i understand. you were talking about your hubbies. i can't
judge you for having multiple husbands. i'm not like that.

FS
But I don't have a husband yet
I'm single
I'm just looking for the right man to be my husband

John
so the other hubbies didn't work out? how many men will it
take?

FS:
You don't understand a single word
There is different between husband and hubbie
Husband is your love

John
they are the same thing.

FS:
Hubbies is what you like to do. Like traveling, swimming,
fishing
Reading, and so on

John
yes, i understand that is why you married your husbands,
because you like to DO them.

FS:
I'm still single
I don't have a husband
Don't you see this

Single means someone who is not married
I'm single

John
i get it. when the hubby is gone, it does get lonely. it's almost
like you are single...

FS:
I don't know how to explain to you again
Ate you married
Are*

John
i ate some married one time. i put some orange sauce on it.
not bad...

FS:
Are you married?

John
for lunch i think three days ago. i don't like it overcooked.

FS:
Don't you know the meaning of married?
John
you asked me if i ate some, i was trying to answer your
question!

      Notice the frustration in the dialogue of the FS. They
are quick-tempered. Patience is apparently not a virtue for
someone who needs crack or heroin right now. A real woman
who was on M with me would never get like that. If she was a
real woman, and I was joking around with her like that she
would be flattered, laughing, making jokes about me, or the
context. A FS can't understand humor in the English
language. They don't have enough fluency. Fluency requires
intense study and work. Dope sick people can't focus on

things like that. They have to use the marginal skills they have, which only gets them through a check out line.

The lines they read and methods they use came from a script from the head guy has written in a scam boiler room operation. This guy has slightly better fluency, and receives a larger portion of the proceeds. He is motivated in this way to communicate in English and he walks back and forth among the rows of men operating profiles of women answering questions about the next move to motivate the moronic American to send money. He knows that the results have their ups and downs. My goal is to make the down as deep as possible. If I can push his operation into the red, the better. If I can get him into jail or any of his cronies, that will put a smile on my face, and it also puts a smile on God's face.

That's why I do what I do: (semicolon intentionally not used here) I can't see God's smile, but one day I will. And that smile is worth any amount of effort. There is no better validation. The thought of putting a smile on God's face brings a tear of joy to my eye. And that tear will not hinder me to see my computer screen which brings up the next FS who is trying to contact me right away.

Also, I believe that most FS are lazy. They hit me up and ask what I do for a living. All my information is on the first page of my profile. Even Ray Charles could see it as plain as day. An FS doesn't have time for that, the basic investigation of their mark. What the method of the FS is to operate with volume, many different chat convos simultaneously, and try to lead a man through a logic maze that ultimately gets him to send her money. The FS knows nothing about American businesses or careers and doesn't want to look that crap up. They see it as a waste of time. It's a critical mistake she makes, the FS who is newly decided to marry me or have unlimited sex with me.

Of course, the "her" is usually a "guy" who sits behind a computer in a boiler room operation across an ocean. Note that they often with "good morning". Usually if an FS opens with "good morning", I am looking at my clock, which reads 11:32 pm. That means the FS is either not fluent, which is impossible for any American or Canadian to make that mistake OR they are careless because they are operating a volume of dialogues with many people. The truth is both cases are correct.

Sometimes I unleashed some brutality, unapologetically:

FS:
Hello

    John
    Hi

    FS:
    How are you doing

    John
    good you?

    FS:
    Am fine
    Where are you from

    John
    where do you live?

    FS:
    Michigan in USA
    You?

    John
    ive never met a woman named (man's name) before
(the picture and profile were typical of the FS)

    FS:
    It normal
    Where are you from

John
yes how can i help?

FS:
How did you which to help me
JUN 17TH, 8:38PM

FS:
Hello
JUN 17TH, 9:46PM

John
a woman named "(man's name)" are you?

FS:
Yes dear
Did you like that

John
are you a tranny?

FS:
No
Why asking that

John
just a random question, no reason

FS:
Okay
What did you do for living

John
What did I do? Well, at my first job I riveted steel for
Bushmills.

FS:

Okay

John
what is the problem?

FS:
Am still single
And you

John
I thought you wanted my resume?

FS:
I don't understand that

John
which part?

FS:
I want your resume as how
(FS often cannot complete sentences in the natural way
an American or Canadian would. This is because it is
unnatural for them because of the conventions of their foreign
language and culture.)

John
well, i was going to tell you about the job requirements
of Bushmills, but if you don't care, i can't force you.

FS:
Okay you can go ahead my dear

John
i mean, if you don't want it, then you don't have to have
it

FS:
I want it

John
ok so one day i was entering through the western entrance, and Bob was there

FS:
Okay

John
So I was asking him about the   10 unit production requirement, because the last hour of the day before, which was a Tuesday...

FS:
Okay

John
this is the cool part

FS:
Okay
That
Nice

John
so we got interrupted
and the arc welder was running low on amperage.

FS:
Okay
John
anyway, sorry. i'm working on a review for Life magazine
we tested it, and we could not get the power right. so they were trying to say production was low for a different reason
you know what i mean of course
right?

FS:
Yes

John
so you know about amps?
hello?
get lost

FS:
Hello
How are you doing

John
hey sucker. i mean (man's name)

FS:
How are you my love
Hope you are really good

John
how's the scam going? i mean being a hairdresser

FS:
What the f*** are saying their

John
i didn't mean to type scam. sorry about that scammer.
what i meant to ask was how is the hairscamdressing going?

FS:
That left to you

John
say what? how's africa over there? i bet it's like a
"boiler room". do you know what a boiler room is?
        get back to me after it takes you two hours to figure it
out, chump

FS:
What is the mean of all this rubbish you saying, who
are you calling a scam
10:34PM

FS:
Hello

John
probably you

FS:
Yes
What are you doing

John
chatting with somebody in a boiler room
man your english is weak

FS:
You talking to your mum i guess

John
no chatting with my mum is not what i said, was it?
as i said, your english sucks
how many marks are you working right now anyway?

FS:
No,i mean you are insulting your generation i guess
living in an hen
No mark

John
haha right
i'm insulting my generation? you pulled that right out of
an ancient phrasebook i guarantee it

FS:
F*** off man

John
yeah? big tough guy
hope you can swim across the atlantic sucker
cause crack addicts and scammers can't afford plane
tickets
even if you were here, i'd still easily take you
dope sick people aren't much for an altercation my
friend
they lack the killer instinct

FS:
That for you
I have a question

John
that for me?
are you in second grade?
you'd have to speak english to ask me a question
sucker
it aint easy is it?

FS:
Can you get me people to scam

John
sure i could. i know a lot of honest people who make
good money.
but will i do that?

FS:
When i scam them we share it equally
I mean the money

John
Haha

FS:
Yes

John
you wouldn't share equally with your own "mum"
you couldn't multiply by 0.5 if your next fix depended on
it

here's a question:

FS:
Yes i will share it for i swear

John
what is 17 times 1/2?
5 seconds
4
3
2
1
fail!
you can't even do that?
pathetic
God is not going to be sad when he condemns you and
your cronies.
and neither will I

FS:
Can you do what i ask you

John
in fact, if Nigeria disappears tomorrow, it will be a good
day for everyone
your country is a toilet

FS:
S***
Can you do what i ask you

John
why are you saying your name right now?

FS:
Give me reasonable to my question

John
i'm good

FS:
Can you get me people to scam
Yes or no

John
already answered moron
i wouldn't introduce you to Hitler.

FS:
Okay

John
you understood that much.
why did you know about hitler but not basic math?

FS:
Hey
Who are you going to give me to scam
Then after scamming him we share the money

John
apparently if i scammed somebody for $17, you can't
do enough math to split it in half, is one problem for you. you
apparently didn't go to school. which means you are probably
stupid.
my intelligence is verified by an international
organization and the military.
but scammers don't read posts, do they?

FS:
Shut your f***ing mouth if you do what i ask you let me
no

John
one of the reasons you can't scam people is because
you can't read
but even if you could read, you would still have a hard
time for other reasons.
the main reason is because you aren't smart anyway.
i gave you a basic math problem to solve and you
couldn't and still haven't

FS:
Okay give me someone who have money ,then you see
maybe i can scam or not

John
ok bill gates. try to scam him
i will send you a dollar if you can scam him, if i have
one that day
and i'm telling you, if you can't scam me, you definitely
cannot scam him.
but realize this, if i seriously thought you were going to
scam bill gates, i'd notify him as soon as i found out.

FS:
Give me your friend that have money or someone
around you

John
that also applies to anybody else

FS
give me your friend? Haha

John

how do i give you my friend?
nice english moron
turd

FS:
F*** you
John
haha
let me have it baby
so you learned to cuss in english, you know hitler might
be bad, but no math?

FS:
I mean give me your friend to scam or people around
you that have money

John
or what?
coming after me are you?
give me your best ultimatum

FS:
Njo
No

John
what would be the best for you is to turn off your
computer and get an honest job.

FS:
You are a f*** up man

John
it's called WORK - look it up donkey
it's the way people earn money and stay out of jail

FS:
I said give someone to scam

John
huh?

FS:
Give me someone to scam

John
i already did idiot
how's it going?
how in the world did you learn to operate a computer?
you don't have the brains to put a fork in your mouth

FS:
F*** you
John
the reason why i won't give you someone to scam is
because i don't help scammers. i hate scams

FS:
Am not in need of the one you gave me
Okay

John
i also hate scammers
you are evil

FS:
I need someone else

John
why would i give you someone else? you didn't work
on the one i gave you
if i gave you a dollar bill, and you threw it in the trash,
should i gave you another?

FS:
Yes give another

John
bro, don't scam people. it's wrong and it's illegal. i don't do it, and won't help any person do it under any conditions.

FS:
Okay
Thanks
But remember it all about Money (I guess the genius was trying to motivate me with that statement or something?)

John
don't overdose on heroin tonight junkie
you can't even read man

FS:
I can see is like you don't need money

John
huh?
try again that didn't make sense in English

FS:
I said, is like you don't need money in your life

John
i really doubt you went to school
what does that even mean man?
the only thing you have learned in english is a script your scam boss gave you

FS:
Ask your mum about that

John
i can't ask my "mum" about jibberish you moron

if you try me in a battle of wits you will lose.

any progress on scamming bill gates, scam boy?

dude if you can't scam me, you can't scam anybody
and that's good.

one less scammer is good for me and good for God
zzzzzz

FS:
Keep that to your self

John
i'm going to sleep now, that is how interesting you are
moron

FS:
I have scam people stupid like you fool

John
change your name to moron

FS:
Okay

John
or change your name to idiot
or donkey
or criminal
or inmate
or junkie

FS:
I have work to do

John

or thief

FS:
Bye fool

John
any or all of those names is what you are

FS:
Idiot

John
i'm the one you couldn't scam
did i send you money? yes or no?
check your account.
is there money in it from me today?
i'll wait while you check your account

FS:
Ask your mum that

John
see if it has money from me or not.

FS:
I f*** are today

John
huh?
nice english
if you were in canada you couldn't ask for the bathroom

FS:
Send your account details then i scam your life
Fool

John

son, you're too stupid to open a door

FS:
Get lot

(he temporarily blocks me, as I write this, and comes back on line to hurt my feelings.)

Hi

John
boy you couldn't walk if you fell out of a boat!

FS:
Fool i get you out
Bye

John
"i get you out"? what does that mean?

FS:
I have work to do

John
you're too lazy to work junkie

(he disappears)

Here's an interesting profile:

(female name here, a first name for the last name)
You're friends on Facebook
Cashier at Walmart Store
Lives in Battle Creek, Michigan

So here's the picture of the Walmart cashier:

It seems like being a cashier is probably paying better than swimsuit modeling right now. Especially if you can get on at the prestigious Walmart in Battle Creek. I have nothing against Walmart, Battle Creek or Michigan. In fact, I actually resent the fact that some person across the Atlantic Ocean are using that information in order to create a scam.

This is the heart of the matter: can I prove that these people are FS? No. What do I know about them? Only what is on their profiles. But when I start to add up all the elements of their profiles and compare these phonies to real people I can verify, I quickly start to smell trouble. FS are lazy, do not fill out profiles, and can't speak English very well. So why is someone like that contacting me out of the blue? There is only one reason: they think I'm rich because I'm an American. They know a lot more than they talk about during our M.

But they usually have to start out with something that they would talk about with a new person in real life. In a small country, there are places in Africa, Asia or South America, where they have encountered someone from a nearby country. When they detected this new stranger's accent, a common question is, "What country are you from?" In America, this is a rarity. Even though we have problems with immigration over here, even if I hear someone who has a distinctive accent from a certain part of America, I usually do not start with "What state are you from?" The reason this makes sense to an FS is because it's a more common question in a smaller country where people traverse across it.

The FS also likes to start off with "What is your marital status". Never a question mark is included, but also this robotic question helps the FS find the most likely victim, a lonely guy. This poor man doesn't currently have a woman in his life, and he searches on F and before long, a beautiful model is interested in him.

Sometimes a scammer gets hot and actually looks up my name, and puts it after hello. This is not a normal thing to do for a young American girl. "Hello" is mainly used by old timers. Women know that in America, they hold all the cards. An American man is faced with this reality every day. It's awful to be a man here. Even though the women here are pretty, they rarely want to be with a man who is not rich or famous. American women worship the dollar as much as the equally-secular Godless men do. Women get to the big dollars here by being pretty, a rich man will not do with less. Women here practice regular hypergamy. That's an ancient way that a woman survives. She finds the wealthiest man, and even after finding a rich man, moves on to another rich man if the next guy is richer – that is, if she's attractive.

Hypergamy has its perils. Usually a woman in America gets a rich guy because she is hot. They rush into the bedroom, she attempts to get pregnant. It usually works. Either she gets pregnant and he pays her, which can happen in or out of court, and is quite lucrative for the woman for 18 years, or she continues to have sex with him until he marries her. Her strategy is to give him a taste, just a whiff of the incredible sex, and withdraw it from him until he presents her a ring. If it's value is proportional to his wealth by her subjective definition, she will marry him – temporarily.

If she gets fat, she can't move on, she clings to him on a permanent basis. If she is still pretty, she pumps out kids for a while. Sometimes a richer guy comes along and sweeps her off of her feet. This whole ordeal is the plight of Godless people. They have no respect for marriage, and women only hang out when they are receiving resources from men. When that gets threatened, they move on if they can. If they can't, they are in big trouble.

Since pretty women hold all the cards in a society that is motivated by money, why would they contact a strange man? They don't. Unless they are a FS. The games continue:

This one's initials were "FS"! I couldn't write this unless I was some kind of writer…wait a second…: (this one is a little dirty, which I don't normally do, but it illustrates the illiteracy of the FS.)

FS makes first contact, in a frantic way:
Hi

FS:
Hi

John
hi. do you want to have a conversation?

FS:
Yes
9:14PM

FS:
Hi

John
what up

FS:
How are you doing?

John
good u?

FS:
Cool
Where are you originally from?

John
a vagina

FS:
Cool

John
have you been there?

FS:
No (not a natural reaction if it was a woman)
What is your marital status

John
it's a nice place. some parts can get hairy
(this foreigner ignores this statement as they don't want
to have to get out their English dictionary and look words up.
What they do is copy the same things over and over again,
expecting a different result. Sounds like the definition of a
word I've heard many times, which is a "scammer".)

FS:
What is your marital status

John
it's good
i like my marital status

102

FS:
Are you single?

John
everyone is unless they are a conjoined twin

FS:
I'm flora from brazoria tx I'm single no kids and never married

John
i'm a conjoined twin

FS:
Can I see your pics?

John
yes take a look (I sent nothing.)

FS:
Okay

John
what do you think? (still, I sent nothing)

FS:
Nothing

John
you didn't like us?

FS:
I love you
If you can trust me
(this is where the FS is trying to put the move on me)

John
i love you too

definitely i trust you
(what an idiot this one is)

FS:
Okay

John
give me one second (I just did this to waste their time a little bit.)

back

FS:
Okay

John
Okay
it's your turn...
well it's been nice knowing you.
i will forever treasure our time together

FS:
Okay

John
stop saying Okay Okay?
(scammer sends pictures, I close out.)

Later I get back on. Little did this scammer know that I knew she either was an American scammer, or a half-way fluent foreign scammer. Either way, the scammer easily cuts to the chase, which is one angle or another. This scammer was working the sympathy angle. Unfortunately, I decided to cut it short. I had what is called "a life".)

This FS makes first contact

Hello John
How are you doing ?

John
Hi

Christine Gonzalez Hughes
I'm Christine

John
and I'm not (the FS as usual knows nothing about this classic Chevy Chase line from Saturday Night Live.)

Christine Gonzalez Hughes
I'm from madera califonia
John
everything you've said so far matches your profile

Christine Gonzalez Hughes
Yea I don't need to lie about anything
Where are you from ?
(since there was a chance that this person might not be in the FS, I decided to check out her profile. She only had around 150 friends, which is light. There were only about 5 posts, another red flag. All this seemed to add up to an American scamjob. I wondered what her angle was. I looked up her town, Madera, CA to see if it even existed. It was there, in what looked like a small, isolated rural part of California. I had an idea to tell her I was from a nearby small town. If she recognized the name, she would acknowledge that. I looked the map over. The city of Fresno was relatively close to Madera. As I zoomed into Fresno, I looked around for an obscure neighborhood. I knew nothing about Clovis, California, but Clovis was the first name that popped up after one or two clicks of a zoom. I had never heard of it, but it was close or within Fresno, so I thought that if she had grown up in Madera, there was a decent chance that she would recognize

that name. That is, if she was real. She neither acknowleged it, nor answered any of my questions satisfactorily. She was quickly rushing me into her angle and saw my questions as a distraction. That the way an addict is: they don't care about you or your life unless it helps them gain information on how they can get money from you. Had she looked at my profile, she would have had ample opportunity to figure out that I was not from California. A normal person wanting a relationship would call that out for what it is. She instead tried to move me through her process.)

John
Clovis

FS
I work as interior decorating (bad grammar, another earmark of a non-American)

John
where are you located?

FS
Currently in Texas
Am 30yrs old (no American starts a sentence with Am. It's unnatural.)

John
what part of texas?

FS
Caldwell (so I had an American scammer on my hands. That's disheartening. My own people. I had lost an uncle in Vietnam and my grandpa got shot and was awarded the Bronze Star for bravery during WWII for these pieces of excrement.)

John
what do you do there?

FS
With my sister
She's disable
So am helping her till I get any project to do

John
that's not a career
did you go to college?

FS
Yea sure

John
which one, what major?

FS
Madera college of education (not likely. Madera looked like the town was too small, even to support a community college.)

John
what was the name of your dormatory?

(FS disappears)

Scamming scammers was a bit of fun. I'll probably continue it once in a while. The reason I can't do it full time is because it doesn't contain a paycheck, and doesn't impact crime very much. Of course, I want to impact crime. If I could find a way to make a deeper impression into the seedy intent of the evildoers, I would. For me unfortunately, the biggest act I could do is to waste the time of the low-level pickpockets for a brief season. I couldn't get to the higher up bosses that run the scams. There are ways to do that, but it's not easy, and I discovered there is a whole community of people who do it as a sport.

The sport is called "scam baiting". At this point, since I am not a professional, I have to exit stage right and leave the rest to the professionals at 419eater.com. It looks like a fun hobby, but I cannot commit to it. I wish everyone well. Thank you for reading. Keep this in mind: if someone's asking you for money, it's a scam. God bless!